The Global Marketplace

Making the Trade

Stocks, Bonds, and Other Investments

Aaron Healey

www.raintreepublishers.co.uk
Visit our website to find out more information about Raintree books.

To order:
☎ Phone 0845 6044371
🖹 Fax +44 (0) 1865 312263
📧 Email myorders@raintreepublishers.co.uk

Customers from outside the UK please telephone +44 1865 312262

Raintree is an imprint of Capstone Global Library Limited, a company incorporated in England and Wales having its registered office at 7 Pilgrim Street, London, EC4V 6LB – Registered company number: 6695582

Text © Capstone Global Library Limited 2011
First published in hardback in 2011
Paperback edition first published in 2012
The moral rights of the proprietor have been asserted.

Edited by Adam Miller and Andrew Farrow
Designed by Ryan Frieson
Original illustrations © Capstone Global Library 2011
Illustrated by Planman Technologies (India) Pvt Ltd
Maps by Mapping Specialists Ltd
Picture research by Hannah Taylor
Originated by Capstone Global Library Ltd
Printed and bound in China by South China Printing Company Ltd

ISBN 978 0 431 00996 4 (hardback)
14 13 12 11 10
10 9 8 7 6 5 4 3 2 1

ISBN 978 1 4062 2042 1 (paperback)
15 14 13 12 11
10 9 8 7 6 5 4 3 2 1

British Library Cataloguing in Publication Data
A full catalogue record for this book is available from the British Library.

Acknowledgements

The author and publisher are grateful to the following for permission to reproduce copyright material: Alamy Images p. **34** (© les polders); Corbis pp. **35** (Craig Pulsifer), **43** (Eleanor Bentall), **44** (epa/Justin Lane), **47** (Reuters/Larry Downing), **48** (Minnesota Historical Society); Corbis SABA p. **27** (Greg Smith); Getty Images pp. **25** (Bloomberg/Daniel Acker), **30** (Jim Bourg); Photolibrary pp. **4** (age fotostock/Casey Kelbaugh), **6** (Radius Images), **8** (Rafael Macia), **12**, **14** (Jean-Pierre Boutet), **18** (Creatas), **41** (Blend Images/Andersen Ross); Rex Features p. **10** (Edward Webb).

Cover photograph of the trading floor of the New York Stock Exchange, March 2008, reproduced with permission of Getty Images (Scott Wintrow).

We would like to thank Michael Miller and Laura J. Hensley for their invaluable help in the preparation of this book.

Every effort has been made to contact copyright holders of any material reproduced in this book. Any omissions will be rectified in subsequent printings if notice is given to the publisher.

All the Internet addresses (URLs) given in this book were valid at the time of going to press. However, due to the dynamic nature of the Internet, some addresses may have changed, or sites may have changed or ceased to exist since publication. While the author and publisher regret any inconvenience this may cause readers, no responsibility for any such changes can be accepted by either the author or the publisher.

Contents

Some words are printed in bold, **like this**. You can find out what they mean by looking in the glossary.

A world of investment

If you use your time to read this book, what is in it for you? You hope that by putting your time into reading it, you will gain useful knowledge in return. Your decision to read this book is an **investment** of your time.

As with any investment, you are taking a **risk**. You are betting and hoping that reading this book will be time well spent. If you do not learn anything, you will know that you have made a bad bet. The time you spent will be lost, and the chance to do other things with your time – such as watching a film or hanging out with friends – will be gone as well.

Risks and rewards

Just as you take a risk when you decide where to **invest** your time, people take risks when they decide to invest their money. The world is full of opportunities for investing money. Each carries its own risks and rewards.

Some kinds of investments carry less risk, such as putting money into a **savings** account. The chances of losing the money are very small, but you will also make less money. Other kinds of investments are riskier, such as putting money into a new business. You will lose your money if the business does not succeed. But if the business becomes a multimillion-pound success, then you stand to make a lot of money.

With every investment decision comes a hidden cost. This is the cost of not being able to invest the money in another way or to spend it on something else, because you already used your money for the investment. This cost is known as the opportunity cost.

It may not seem fair, but working is the only risk-free way of making money!

Easy money?

If you have worked at a job, then you may have already wished that there could be an easier way to make money. Making money is usually not easy. It takes hard work and lots of time. But investing offers the promise of making money quickly, with little effort. That is why people look for ways to invest their money to make more money. Of course, if people make unwise investments, all their hard-earned money can be lost.

Investment choices

As technology spreads and the world becomes more interconnected, the opportunities for investing money increase. In this book, you will learn about the ways people are investing their money around the world today, and the risks and rewards available at every turn.

It might seem as though you will never save enough money to invest. But someday, with luck and hard work, you will be able to make choices about where to invest your money. This table shows some of the many investment options available to people.

DIFFERENT KINDS OF INVESTMENTS	
Form of investment	**What it does**
Current account (page 14)	Keeps money conveniently available, but it may not earn any money
Instant access savings account (page 15)	Money can be withdrawn when you need it, but it earns money slowly
Notice savings account (page 16)	Money makes more interest than in an instant access savings account, but there is a notice period for withdrawal
ISA (page 16)	A certain amount of money can be saved in an Individual Savings Account (ISA) every year free of tax
Savings bond (page 22)	A lump sum can be saved in a savings bond, often at a guaranteed rate of interest, for a fixed period of time
Share (page 24)	These small units of ownership of companies can earn or lose money
Unit trust (page 24)	These are mixed groups of shares sold together as units
Property (page 32)	Property usually rises in value over a long period of time, but values can fall, too. There are also costs involved in buying and selling property, and your money can get tied up in a property that doesn't sell.
Commodities such as gold, oil, or wheat (page 35)	Value can rise or fall due to world events that affect supply and demand

The market for money

As the chart on page 5 shows, there are many different kinds of investments. They are all part of the world financial **markets**.

A market is a system that allows people to trade one thing for another. There are many kinds of markets, for everything from cotton to houses. Items such as cotton and houses are "**goods**", or items of **value**, that can be bought and sold. The **price** (amount charged) is determined by what buyers are willing to pay for it, and what sellers are willing to sell it for.

Where are markets located?

People tend to think of markets as having one physical location. This is often the case, such as when we go to a shoe shop where buyers and sellers interact, or to a bank where borrowers and savers go to do business.

But markets do not have to be located in any particular place. For example, people have bought goods from catalogues for years without leaving home. Buying and selling from home is becoming even more common today thanks to the Internet. Whether you live in the United States, United Kingdom, Argentina, South Africa, or South Korea, you can buy and sell almost anything on auction websites, such as eBay.

Markets exist anywhere and anytime people interact with each other by buying and selling goods or **services** (acts performed for a fee) at mutually agreeable prices.

Shopping centres are a kind of market.

The language of money

Terms such as *money*, **income**, *wealth*, and *net worth* are often used when discussing finances. What does each of these terms mean, and how are they different?

Money

Money is how people pay for the things they want, and it includes cash, cheques, and debit cards. It is a way to create exchanges or to make payments. In the United Kingdom, money is counted in pounds. The United states has the dollar, Japan has the yen, and euros are used in many European countries.

Money is also a method for measuring the market value of goods and services. For example, the amounts that people charge for services such as babysitting, walking a neighbour's dog, or washing a car show what the current value is of that service.

Income

Income is how much money you earn from your job (sometimes called a salary or wage), or from gifts and pocket money. It can also be the money you make from investments.

Wealth and net worth

The terms *wealth* and *net worth* are often used to mean the same thing. Net worth is the market value (potential selling price) of your **assets** (items of value) minus your **debts** (money owed) on a given date. If your only asset is a computer system worth £1,500, but you owe a debt to someone of £1,000, then your net worth is positive – £500. If your debt is greater than the worth of your assets, then you have a negative net worth. Of course, you should always try to make sure that your net worth is positive!

Financial markets

Financial markets are like other markets – but in these markets, money is what is "bought" and "sold". Financial markets are all around us. People can invest money from almost anywhere in the world by making a deposit in a savings account electronically (see pages 14 and 15), or buying **shares** and **bonds** over the Internet (see pages 18 to 31). Or people can borrow money from almost anywhere by using a **credit** card to make a purchase.

Joining the financial markets

You may not realize it, but when you put money in the bank or building soceity or make another financial investment, you become part of the financial markets.

For example, when you put money in a savings account, you are temporarily "selling" your money to the bank. You might look for a bank that will pay you the most **interest**, which is the additional money you get for agreeing to place your savings with the bank.

Banks, in turn, lend out your money to people around the world, using **loans** (money given with repayment conditions), credit cards, and other means. But they do not simply give people all the money they ask for. In addition to the money they give, they charge interest. This extra money helps keep banks in business.

If nobody invested their money, businesses would not have money available for major projects like the Burj Khalifa in Dubai, the world's tallest building.

Fuelling the global marketplace

If banks did not take in savings, they would not be able to offer loans to people, including businesses. And if people did not invest in other kinds of financial products like shares (also known as stocks) and bonds, this would further prevent businesses from getting money.

What would happen if no one invested their money? Businesses around the world would eventually stop working. They would not have the money to develop and introduce new products, build new buildings, buy necessary equipment, or hire new workers. Because of this lack of money, businesses would need to lay off workers.

In addition to losing their jobs, people would suffer in other ways if everyone stopped investing. Banks would not be able to offer loans, and without loans many families would not be able to buy new cars and houses, or make home improvements.

In these ways, the money that people invest is the fuel that keeps the global marketplace running. Without investment and healthy financial markets, world **economies** would collapse (see box below).

The credit crunch

In 2008 and 2009, the world got a taste of what life would be like if financial markets were not working. During this period, banks suddenly stopped lending much money. It happened because banks around the world had offered loans to too many people who could not repay them. These loans had been traded to other banks around the world until nobody was sure just who had these "bad" loans.

Because of the loans, banks began to run out of money. Even when banks had money to lend, because of their recent bad experiences, many banks became afraid of lending money. Many people began taking their money out of banks and other investments. This lack of available money became known as "the credit crunch".

The entire world economy seemed to be in danger of collapse. People worried that once banks could not borrow money from each other, or businesses could not get finance, they would quickly fail. To prevent disaster, the governments in the most affected countries loaned billions to banks and other financial institutions to ensure they had enough money. The situation improved, but lending remained slow for more than a year.

Bringing people together

As you've just learned, investing keeps the economy moving. People who have money to invest look for ways to make the most of their money. Meanwhile, businesses are eager to receive these investments to help them grow. To achieve these goals, **investors** (people who invest money) and businesses meet in the financial markets.

Financial markets co-ordinate the amount that savers want to save with the amount that people such as businesses want to borrow. They do much the same thing for savings that other markets do for shoes, jewellery, toothpaste, and other products.

Supply and demand

Consider the market for a common product, such as shoes. Every day individuals, called **consumers**, in countries throughout the world plan on buying a pair of shoes in their size. They create a **demand** for shoes. Meanwhile, a smaller (but still large) number of individuals, called **producers**, throughout the world are making plans to produce and distribute shoes. They are creating the **supply** of shoes.

Have you ever had a hard time finding a certain pair of trainers? If so, the demand for that style was greater than the supply.

Producers cannot possibly check with everyone interested in buying shoes to find out what they want to buy. Yet, if the number of shoes consumers plan on buying is greater than the number producers plan on selling, there will be a shortage of shoes. As a result, some buyers will not find the shoes they want. And if the number of shoes consumers plan on buying is fewer than the number producers plan on selling, producers will have a surplus of shoes. This means they will have too many left over.

Finding an equilibrium point

Fortunately, the market helps to solve problems like this. It does so by affecting prices. The price is set by supply and demand.

When consumers want more shoes than producers are willing to supply at the current price, the market price for shoes will increase. The supply is not meeting the demand, and so consumers have to pay more if they really want the shoes. Similarly, when more producers want to sell shoes at the current price, but there is not enough demand to buy them all, then the market price for shoes will decrease. Producers will have to be willing to charge less money if they want to sell all of their shoes.

The market price will reach the point at which consumers' plans to buy shoes and producers' plans to sell shoes meet at the same point, known as the equilibrium point (see diagram below).

The same type of price changes bring together buyers and sellers in markets for thousands of different products. Buyers decide how many shoes, toothbrushes, CDs, DVDs, books, or meals they want at the current prices. This interaction between consumers and producers is known as the law of supply and demand. It is markets at work.

This diagram shows how the needs of consumers and producers meet at a point known as the equilibrium point.

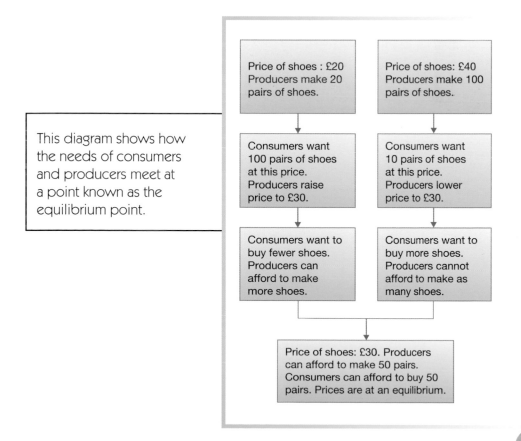

Price of shoes : £20
Producers make 20 pairs of shoes.

Price of shoes: £40
Producers make 100 pairs of shoes.

Consumers want 100 pairs of shoes at this price. Producers raise price to £30.

Consumers want 10 pairs of shoes at this price. Producers lower price to £30.

Consumers want to buy fewer shoes. Producers can afford to make more shoes.

Consumers want to buy more shoes. Producers cannot afford to make as many shoes.

Price of shoes: £30. Producers can afford to make 50 pairs. Consumers can afford to buy 50 pairs. Prices are at an equilibrium.

Financial markets at work

As with markets for shoes, financial markets find a balance among the needs of different groups. Just as the shoe market makes the price of shoes consistent, the financial markets make the plans of savers and borrowers consistent with each other.

Investing in Henry Ford

US inventor Henry Ford (1863–1947) had a knack for taking things apart and putting them back together again. Growing up, he earned money fixing his neighbours' watches and almost anything mechanical he could get his hands on. He got a job as an engineer at the Edison Illuminating Company in 1891. But Ford wanted to produce automobiles. Most importantly, he wanted to make cars that offered better quality at a lower price than his competitors, so that everyone could afford to buy one.

Luckily, investors believed in Ford and his innovations, so they gave him the money he needed to turn his innovative ideas into goods that ordinary people could afford to buy. With this money, Ford was able to produce equipment that significantly improved the speed at which his cars were built – the moving conveyor belt, for example. Ford had a dream, and he succeeded. It brought him wealth and fame. But had it not been for investors and their willingness to bet on his ideas, Ford would have been like thousands of people throughout history who never had the chance to make their dreams come true.

By 1911 Ford cars were being produced in Manchester at the company's first British factory.

Unlike the shoe market, where prices are listed in pounds, the "price" that brings savers and borrowers together is the **interest rate**. This is the price that people pay over time for the chance to borrow money. It is also the amount that you earn if you "lend" the money to a bank by putting it in a savings account.

When interest rates are higher, people are more likely to put money in savings. This is because they will earn more interest on the money they invest. When interest rates are lower, people are more likely to borrow. This is because borrowing is less expensive when there is a low interest rate. The needs of different people eventually lead to an interest rate that keeps the financial markets moving forward.

Investing for the future
When the needs of savers and borrowers are co-ordinated well, the market for borrowing money works smoothly. People and businesses with good ideas are able to get loans to build new businesses. They can also use investment money to find better ways to produce existing products and to create completely new products.

These investments may turn what seem like impossible dreams to one generation into conveniences the next generation takes for granted. Everything from mobile phones to medicines to cars and aeroplanes are the result of inventors' ability to borrow in the financial markets (see box at left). We all benefit today from investments that have been made in education, research, machinery, and equipment.

Risks and drawbacks
While such investments have great potential for improving people's lives, they are also risky. Many impossible dreams really are impossible. And even if they are eventually realized, it may be after years of failures and tremendous financial **losses** for those who invested in such high-potential, high-risk projects.

Even if investment is adding to the world's wealth and advancement, it does not always lead to happiness for everyone. New technologies may lead to workers being fired because they are no longer needed. For example, as car factories use more technology to make and assemble car parts, fewer factory workers are needed, and people lose their jobs. Yet at the same time, new technology can lead to new jobs that workers must be retrained for.

Investments are full of potential risks and rewards. The greater the risk, the higher the possible reward.

Basic investment options

The financial markets offer a variety of investment options, depending on an investor's needs and goals. Each type of investment has its own risks and rewards.

The major categories of financial products that an average investor will come in contact with – and which we will examine in the coming chapters – are **demand deposits**, savings accounts, savings bonds, and shares.

Demand deposits

Current accounts and different types of savings account are all types of demand deposits. The key feature of demand deposits is that the investor can withdraw money from their account at any time, on "demand". Because your money is readily accessible, compared to other financial products, demand deposits have the lowest risks. However, because of this there is also a lower reward, or **return**. With low or no interest being paid, earnings are small.

Automated teller machines (ATMs) are a quick and easy way to access money you have in a current account.

Current accounts

People open current accounts in banks or building societies mainly for the convenience of being able to pay bills by cheque, **standing order**, **direct debit**, or by debit card. Most bank customers do not open current accounts with the goal of making money. The **depositor** receives little or no interest and may even have to pay a service fee. For this reason most financial experts do not consider current accounts to be an investment.

Putting money in a current account is like making a loan to your bank or building society. This is true of all the accounts where money is deposited that are discussed in this chapter. The bank or building society can then make its own loans.

Instant access savings accounts

A common way of saving money is by making deposits in an instant access savings account. Compared to current accounts, which have little risk and little or no reward, this type of savings account pays out interest on your savings.

Depositing money in an instant access savings account is also a kind of loan to the bank or building society. In return for this, interest is paid on the money that is deposited according to the terms of the account. The money is then used by the bank or building society to make loans to borrowers who want to invest in businesses, or who need money for big purchases, such as a house or a car. The bank or building society charges more to the individuals who take out loans than it pays out to depositors with savings accounts. This is how financial institutions make money.

With an instant access savings account, your money is available whenever you want to take it out. Because of this convenience to you as a depositor, a lower interest rate is paid than on some other types of deposit accounts.

How do interest rates work?

Remember the laws of supply and demand in the example of the shoe market? (See pages 10 and 11.) The price for shoes was set by supply and demand. The same thing happens with borrowers and savers in the financial markets.

If too many people want to save or lend money at the going interest rate, and not enough people want to borrow it, the interest rate will go down. As a result, the demand for borrowing money increases. If the interest rate is so low that lots of people want to borrow money, but not many people want to save or lend, interest rates will tend to rise.

Notice savings accounts

Another form of savings account is the notice account that offers a higher rate of interest than an instant access savings account, but has restrictions. For example, some notice accounts require that a minimum amount of money be in the account at all times. Others require that the money remain untouched for a set amount of time, or that a week or even a month's notice is given before money can be withdrawn. With most of these accounts the money can be accessed if absolutely necessary, but there might be a fee to be paid, or all the interest paid might be lost.

Because of the restrictions on notice savings accounts, the bank or building society has more freedom to use and make a profit out of the money that is deposited. As a result, these accounts have a higher rate of interest than instant access savings accounts.

ISAs

An ISA is a Individual Savings Account. Under UK government regulations in 2010, a saver could deposit up to £10,200 in a cash ISA every year and does not have to pay income tax on the interest earnings. These accounts are very popular with tax payers, but it is always possible that the rules could change in the future. However, as long as ISAs are available, having a fixed interest rate and no tax payable on earnings seems a good way to save money.

There is also a form of ISA, called a stocks and shares ISA, where the saver buys company shares for their ISA investment. Like all shares accounts, the value can go down as well as up, so this form of ISA is more risky.

Child Trust Fund

From 2002 the UK government introduced a savings and investment account for children, called the Child Trust Fund (CTF). Newborn children from September of that year received a £250 voucher to start their CTF savings account. The account belongs to the child and cannot be accessed until he or she turns 18.

Additional money can be added to the account every year by parents, relatives, or friends. Money in the account, and any gains or income it makes, is tax free. Until autumn 2010, the government put in another £250 voucher when the child turned 7 years old. Once money is deposited it cannot be withdrawn until the child reaches 18 and then only by the child.

In 2010 the UK government announced plans to reduce, then later end, government contributions to these funds. Those who already have a CTF will retain their savings.

Weighing risk and return

The risk-return pyramid shown here illustrates the types of bank and time deposit accounts discussed in this chapter. The higher-risk investments higher up on the pyramid also offer the greatest rewards. With any investment plan, there is always a trade-off between risk and return on investment. This makes choosing the right investment more complicated. Should you just choose the financial product that gives the higher interest rate? Not necessarily. Those accounts that offer higher interest rates also have their own risks and drawbacks.

For instance, notice savings accounts, which are a time deposit, provide a greater interest return than a demand deposit like an instant access savings account or a current account, but there is also a greater risk for two reasons. First, the money in a notice savings account is less available to the investor than money in a demand account. What if you have a financial emergency and need the money? At the very least, you will lose the interest you have earned, but you may also have to pay an early finish penalty, so you could really be out of pocket.

Second, with some notice savings accounts, you agree to a set interest rate for the term of the deposit. If the interest rates then go up, you have lost your chance to invest your money in a savings account at that higher rate. But you could end up ahead with a fixed rate. Even if the interest rates start to fall, you will still get the higher rate that you agreed to.

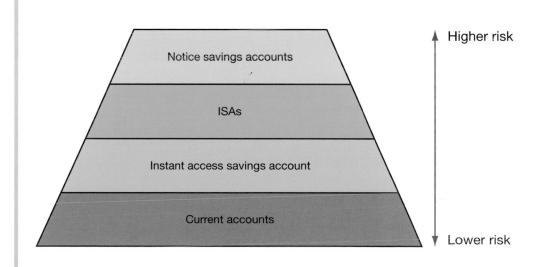

Bonds

There are financial products that offer a better return on investment than bank deposits and time deposits. Of course, the risk is higher, too. One such financial product is bonds.

What is a bond?

When an investor buys a bond, they are loaning money to the organization that sold it – usually a public company or national government. A bond pays a specified interest rate until a stated date of **maturity**. This means that the investor receives money from interest at regular intervals over the course of the year. Then, when the bond reaches its maturity date, the investor also receives back the full amount originally loaned (the principal).

When bonds are bought, the buyer might receive a certificate like these American ones. Certificates list details such as the bond amount and the maturity date.

For example, if the investor buys a £5,000 bond that pays 5 percent a year and matures in 10 years, he or she will receive £250 a year (5 percent of £5,000) for 10 years, and then at the 10-year mark the £5,000 will be returned. If it is a £10,000 bond that pays 6 percent a year and matures in 10 years, the investor will receive £600 a year (6 percent of £10,000) for 10 years, and then the £10,000 will be returned at the 10-year mark. If the investor saves and invests the £250 or £600 interest received in income every year, even more could be earned.

Bond prices and interest rates

Most types of bonds have maturity dates that tell you when the principal will be repaid. However, a bondholder does not have to wait that long to get money back. Bonds can also be bought and sold on active bond markets (see box on page 20). The problem is that the investor may not be able to sell his or her bond for as much as was paid for it because of the changes in interest rates.

How does a changing interest rate affect the price of a bond? If interest rates increase after a bond is bought, then people will be able to find a bond that pays a higher rate. As a result, an investor may find that his or her bond is no longer worth as much for resale. On the other hand, if interest rates decline, the price will increase. People will pay more for the chance to earn the higher interest rate that the bond earns.

Interest rates and public debt

In recent years, many governments have found themselves falling deeper into debt. For example, the United States owes more than US$12 trillion in debt – or more than US$60,000 per person. In the United Kingdom, the total national debt reached about 55 percent of what the country produces in a year.

In order to pay their expenses, these governments issue financial products, such as bonds, which promise to pay the holder in the future, in exchange for their investment today. Government bonds are bought by individual investors, such as retirees, who wish to have very safe investments. These investors know that governments usually do not **default**, or fail to repay (see page 21). Government bonds in one country are also bought by other countries. The Chinese government alone owns nearly US$1 trillion worth of US government bonds.

Selling bonds helps fill a government's immediate need for money. As governments fall deeper into debt, they try to sell more bonds and similar financial products. But if there are not enough people willing to invest in these products, interest rates will rise. As a result, governments will end up owing people even more interest on top of the countries' existing debt. The only way to reverse this situation is to start paying off government debt.

Maturing bonds

The price you can get for a bond is affected by more than just changing interest rates. It is also affected by how soon the bond will mature. In general, the shorter the time until the maturity date, the less likely it is that the bond's price will change.

WHAT IT MEANS TO ME **How a bond works**

Imagine that on 1 September 2009, an investor bought a three-year bond for £1,000 at an interest rate of 3 percent. She will receive an interest payment every six months. At the date of maturity, she will be paid back the amount of her investment. For the three-year bond, the maturity date is 1 September 2012. She will earn £15 every six months, or a total of £90, on her £1,000 investment. (See diagram below.)

What if the investor tried to sell the bond in April 2010? Whoever she sells it to will have a long wait until the investment is repaid, but will make £15 every six months along the way. If interest rates go up and the person could buy a bond with a higher interest rate, then he or she will not be willing to pay the full price (£1,000) for this bond. The person might only pay £980. But if interest rates go down, then the 3 percent rate will look pretty good, and the investor may be willing to pay more.

What if the investor sells her bond in March of 2012? Since there is only one interest payment left and the investment will soon be repaid, the interest rate does not matter much. It will probably sell it for close to £1,000.

| | £15 | £15 | £15 | £15 | £15 | Final interest payment plus principal is £1,015 |

| Buy £1,000 bond on 1 September 2009 | 1 March 2010 | 1 Sept. 2010 | 1 March 2011 | 1 Sept. 2011 | 1 March 2012 | Maturity date: 1 September 2012 |

For example, if a bond with a face value of £10,000 matures tomorrow (meaning the owner will receive the final £10,000 payment tomorrow), its price will be very close to £10,000. The interest rate will not matter much because the bond will not earn much interest before it matures. For this reason, short-term bonds are usually less risky than long-term bonds. Because they are considered less risky, short-term bonds usually pay lower interest.

Bond risks

While bonds are considered "safe" investments, they are not a sure thing. When an investor buys a bond, he or she is loaning money, usually to a business or a government. As with any loan, there is a risk that the interest promised will not be paid, or that the full amount of the money loaned will not be returned.

This risk is very small in the case of bonds issued by governments with stable economies. The risk is a little greater with bonds issued by the governments of countries with less stable economies. The risk is somewhat greater still with major companies with solid credit ratings, and even higher with bonds issued by companies with serious financial problems, or new businesses with unknown prospects.

Bond defaults

The risk of a government defaulting on its debts may seem slim, but it can happen. In 2001 the government of Argentina defaulted on the bonds it had issued to people around the world. Argentina owed bondholders about US$95 billion, and its money reserves were almost gone. People saw the money they had invested for the future disappear.

Other governments tried to force Argentina to repay its debts. In the end, Argentina made a deal to trade the bonds that people held for new bonds that were worth only about one-third of the original value. Many bondholders were angry, but they had little choice, and most agreed to the deal.

This again shows the connection between risk and return. Bonds issued by stable governments typically pay low interest rates because they are the safest investment. The highest interest rates on bonds are paid on those issued by new companies with uncertain prospects. These companies' uncertain futures increase the risk that they will default on interest payments or on the repayment of the bond.

Mutual funds

Many people invest in **mutual funds** that contain many bonds. A mutual fund is a group of investments made by a financial services company on behalf of many investors. A mutual fund manager will choose a set of bonds that appear to be good investments. Investors can place money in the fund. These funds have varying levels of risk and return. Some mutual funds contain only bonds, whereas others contain shares, which are more risky. Bond mutual funds provide a consistent investment return with less risk than investing in shares. For this reason, bond mutual funds are popular among conservative investors who do not want high-risk investments.

Savings bonds

Banks and building societies offer savings bonds to their customers. Most savings bonds give investors a fixed rate of interest for their savings, with no risk to the bond lump sum. But there are two big differences between a savings bond and other savings. First, the investor can't access the money during the term of the bond or sell it on, so it is for long-term investments only. Second, most savings bonds do not let the investor add any more deposits to the original amount invested.

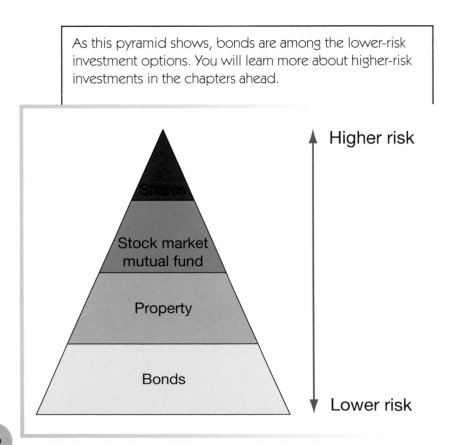

As this pyramid shows, bonds are among the lower-risk investment options. You will learn more about higher-risk investments in the chapters ahead.

Higher risk

Shares

Stock market mutual fund

Property

Bonds

Lower risk

National Savings and Investments

In the United Kingdom there are a series of financial products available through National Savings and Investments (NS&I). These are all backed by HM treasury and investors have no risk to their original capital investment. From time to time, NS&I offers bonds to investors, including guaranteed equity bonds, guaranteed income bonds, and guaranteed growth bonds. NS&I also has other products, such as savings accounts and ISAs.

Premium bonds are a form of investment which are part of the NS&I. Each bond costs £1 and the minimum amount an investor can purchase is £100 worth. The maximum is £30,000. Instead of the investors receiving a fixed or variable interest rate on their premium bond investments, the unique number on every bond is entered in a monthly computerized draw, where the investor can win tax-free sums ranging from £25 to £1 million. At any time, premium bonds can be surrendered for their original value. You could say that owning premium bonds is like having a permanent lottery ticket.

Credit agencies in crisis

Did **credit rating agencies** cause the financial crisis and global **recession** (severe economic downturn) that began in 2008? Some people have argued that they played a large role.

In the late 2000s, investment companies began to offer new types of investments. They included groups of home loans (**mortgages**) that had been bought from banks and packaged together. Many of these mortgages were made to buyers who were at risk of defaulting on the loans (see pages 32 and 33). However, credit rating agencies gave these new investments high credit ratings. Since many people did not understand what was included in these complicated new investments, they trusted the rating agencies and bought them, believing they were safe.

Questioning the agencies

When borrowers began to default on their loans, and the investments people had made therefore failed, the public and the media began to look at the credit agencies more closely. Some people said that the agencies were too slow to lower ratings. Others said they had a close relationship with the companies offering the investments, so they were not giving honest, objective reports.

When it became clear that the investments were risky, credit agencies quickly lowered the ratings of many investments. This caused a panic that made many individuals and businesses afraid of investing at all. The unwillingness to lend or invest deepened the crisis. Many people came to believe that credit agencies need to change the way they rate investments.

Shares

The stock market allows people to easily buy and sell shares. But what is a share? A share is a small unit of ownership of a business. For example, when you buy shares in Apple Computers, you become a part-owner of that company. Depending on what you buy, you will probably only own a small amount of the company. Hundreds or even thousands of other shareholders own the company alongside you. There are also institutional investors. These are organizations with huge supplies of cash (like banks and retirement funds). They invest this cash into company shares.

Risks and rewards

When you buy shares in a company, you share in its risks and rewards. If business is good, the value of the company will rise, and your share price will rise along with it. When things go wrong, share prices will drop. And if the company goes out of business, your shares may be worthless.

As a part-owner of the business, however, you can have a say in how the company performs. Shareholders can attend meetings and contribute to important decisions. Businesses must work in the interests of the shareholders. Your voice is likely to be a small one, but it is a voice.

Is the shareholder always right?

Some people have criticized the role shareholders play in business decisions. Shareholders often have only one goal in mind: making the value of their shares as high as possible. This means making the company as profitable as possible – sometimes at a cost.

For example, shareholders might be more willing to lay off workers if it makes the business more profitable. Or they might be willing to move a factory to a poorer country where labour is cheaper and environmental regulations are less strict. Of course, the same dangers are true of privately held companies. It is up to the business owners, whoever they are, to weigh how business decisions affect employees and the world around them.

The stock market

There is not one stock market, but many spread over the world. The New York Stock Exchange on Wall Street is the world's largest. Next is the Tokyo Stock Exchange, followed by the London Stock Exchange, which is the oldest stock exchange. Other stock exchanges exist around the world, from Ghana in Africa to Mumbai in India. The United States is home to two other major stock markets: the American Stock Exchange (for smaller companies) and the NASDAQ (for technology-based companies).

The trading floor

Most stock markets have a trading floor—a large room where people gather to make trades. The stock market trading floor is a hectic and noisy place. At the New York Stock Exchange, a bell rings to open and close trading for the day. Shares are traded through a series of steps. Investors call stockbrokers to ask them to buy or sell shares. Here is what happens when a broker receives an order to buy shares:

1. The stockbroker calls his or her floor clerk, who is on the trading floor.

2. The trading clerk tells a floor trader about the order.

3. The floor trader finds another floor trader who is willing to buy or sell the shares. They agree on a price and the sale is made.

4. The final price is relayed back to the trading clerk, who passes on the information to the stockbroker, who alerts the buyer that the deal has been made.

Electronic trades

Today, more and more shares are being traded electronically. The NASDAQ is the world's first electronic stock market, and it has no trading floor. Everything is done remotely on computers.

The stock market floor is a noisy place where floor traders buy and sell shares on behalf of investors.

Investing in shares

Investing in a a public company by buying its shares is generally considered a greater risk than buying a bond. As a part-owner, you get no promises on the return you can expect from holding shares, or how much you will be able to sell them for in the future.

With luck, your shares will pay **dividends**. These are payments public companies sometimes offer to shareholders as a part of a company's **profits** (the total money made on top of costs). However, dividends are not always paid on public company shares. More significant is the rise or fall of the value of the shares – which matters when you decide to sell.

Appreciation and depreciation

If the public company is more profitable than expected, or if investors expect it to become more profitable, then the shares will **appreciate** in value (their price will increase). But if the company is less profitable than expected, or if investors expect it to be less profitable, then the shares will **depreciate** in value (their price will fall). If the company fails, the money from any assets sold – buildings, land, even furniture – will go to pay bondholders first, before any money is paid to the shareholders.

If there is not enough to pay the bondholders the amount they have loaned the company, then the shareholders receive nothing, and their shares become worthless. Public company shares are thus riskier than bonds, but they also can provide a greater return on an investment.

Investing in individual shares

There are several ways to invest in public company shares. The first is to buy shares of an individual company. This is risky, though. Because of the **volatility** (changeability) in the value of any given shares, the value of your investment will be highly uncertain.

The price of shares in a single company can drop significantly because of unexpected events. For example, the price of an airline's shares can drop because its pilots go on a long strike or the price of fuel becomes very high. If a car company has to recall a vehicle because of a safety concern, its share price will drop. However, the price of shares can also suddenly increase because of unexpected events. If a government changes the law to make it easier for a bank to earn big profits, for example, the shares in banks are likely to rise.

Three employees of the UK NatWest bank served prison sentences for their part in the Enron scandal.

The Enron scandal

One reminder of the danger of investing in a single company's shares came from the Enron scandal. This energy company was hailed as one of the most innovative companies in the world. It grew rapidly, and its share price reached as high as US$90 per share. However, people in the company eventually realized that the profits were not real. The profits were the result of people knowingly misrepresenting the company's financial status. When the value of the shares peaked, executives began to sell their shares – knowing the true story of their finances, and that the share price worth would soon dive as a result.

After executives sold their shares, the share price began to drop. However, executives encouraged people to buy more or hold on to their Enron shares. Many employees had large amounts of money invested in Enron shares and trusted the company. They listened and held onto their investment. Eventually, problems within Enron were revealed, and the company collapsed. The share prices dropped to zero, and many employees lost their retirement savings. Outside investors lost a lot of money, too. They learned all too well the dangers of investing in the shares of a single company.

Hedging your bets

How do investors avoid losing it all when the company they own shares in gets in trouble? They do so by investing in a variety of companies. If investors buy shares in many different corporations in different industries, the risk of losing all of their savings is reduced.

Consider, for example, companies that make umbrellas and companies that make suncream. Instead of buying nothing but shares in an umbrella company, you could reduce the risk of your investments by buying some umbrella shares and some shares in a suncream company. With nothing but umbrella shares, you are likely to see a drop in the value of your investment if it does not rain for a long time and the sun shines brightly. But if you also own suncream shares, the loss in the umbrella shares will be moderated, and may be offset completely, by the rising value of suncream shares.

High risk, high reward

Although buying shares in an individual company puts you at risk of losing your money, there is also an opportunity for huge profits. In 1919, when the Coca-Cola Company began to sell shares, an investor could buy one share for US$40. If that investor held that share until 1 December 2004 (or passed it on to his or her grandchildren), the investment would have been worth US$191,544!

Market ups and downs

Although investing in many different shares is safer than investing in a single company or type of shares, sometimes this plan does not work, either. At times, the whole stock market seems to be going up or down.

Sometimes the market seems to be responding to the day's news. For example, a decision by a **central bank** to lower interest rates might lead to higher share prices, as people believe the new rates will boost the economy. (A central bank is a country's main bank, and it has power to regulate financial matters.) But news of a major military conflict might send share prices lower, as investors worry about business being disrupted.

Usually news only has an effect when it is unexpected. For example, say that people know the economy is doing badly and expect the unemployment rate to rise to 7 percent. Then the government announces that unemployment rose to 6.5 percent instead. This is bad news, but it is not as bad as people expected. As a result, share prices may rise.

Bull and bear markets

When there is a long period during which shares in most companies are rising, it is called a bull market. And when there is a long period during which share prices are declining, it is called a bear market.

For example, the 1990s were a time of a bull market. When shares began to fall in 2000, it marked the beginning of a bear market. Prices began rising again in 2003 – another bull market – and dropped again in the bear market that began in 2008.

Sometimes it is difficult to tell which type of market you are in, as the market often rises one day only to fall the next. For example, look at the graph below. It tracks the US Dow Jones Industrial Average, a collection of shares that many people use to judge the stock market as a whole. Even though shares were rising in late 2001, the bear market had not ended. But people did not know that until 2002, when share prices began to fall again. It is impossible to know for sure whether the market will rise or fall in the future.

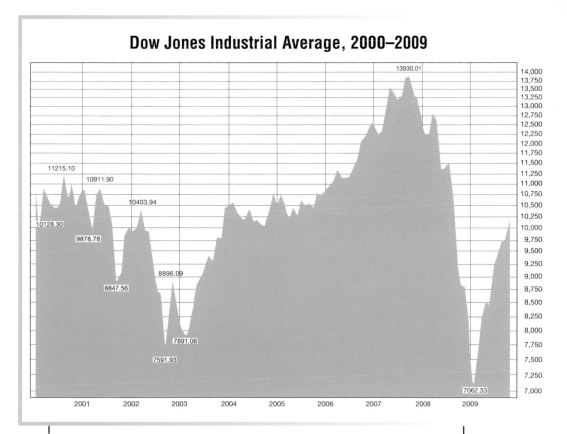

Dow Jones Industrial Average, 2000–2009

This graph shows the US Dow Jones Industrial Average from 2000 through 2009. The stock market dropped dramatically several times during this decade.

Share unit trusts

As with bonds, shares can also be bought in unit trusts. Unit trusts allow people to invest in the shares of thousands of companies with only a small amount of money. Some unit trusts might contain only shares, while others might include bonds, property, gold, and other types of investments.

Unit trusts became popular with ordinary investors in the late 1970s, and their popularity has been growing ever since. There are now thousands of different types offered throughout the world. Unit trusts generally offer a greater return than investors get from bank deposits, time deposits, or bonds, and they are not as risky as buying individual shares.

Managed funds

Most unit trusts are actively run by managers who decide which shares to buy and sell. Managers attract customers who believe the managers can "beat the market". This means they think the managers' wise investments will help them make more money than the stock market as a whole can offer at the time.

Some managers have made millions of pounds by making the right share choices. In the United States, some of these managers, known there as mutual fund managers, are famous in their own right. One of these is Peter Lynch, who ran a famous fund known as the Magellan Fund for 13 years. He was able to pick shares that rose in value by more than 29 percent each year – far better than the stock market average. Does that mean that a good investor should go searching for a good manager before investing? Not necessarily. On average, managers do no better than the market as a whole.

American Peter Lynch became a successful author and speaker after people learned of his skills as a mutual fund manager.

Follow those shares!

It is easy (and can even be fun) to follow the progress of shares. You can start by choosing public companies whose shares are traded on the stock market. Use an Internet site such as www.google.co.uk/finance to track the shares' performance for 10 working days. The table below shows an example of the information you might find.

Col 1	Col 2	Col 3	Col 4	Col 5	Col 6	Col 7
52-WK HI LO	SHARE (SYM)	DIV & YLD	P/E	VOL	CLOSE	CHG
39.04 24.81	ABC	0.76 (2.00%)	16.81	475,966	38.37	-0.27 (-0.70%)
9.75 4.12	FHG	0.17 (2.15%)	23.22	15,404,965	7.84	+0.05 (+0.64%)

Column 1: This reports the highest and lowest share price during the most recent 52-week period.

Column 2: This shows the stock market symbol used for a share. For example, the symbols shown here are for the made-up companies Acme Balloon Company (ABC) and the Fine Hotel Group (FHG).

Column 3: This shows the dividends (DIV), or the annual payment per share to owners. If a dividend is paid, it is usually paid every three months (quarterly). It also shows the yield (YLD), which is the rate of return on a stockholder's investment. It is calculated by dividing the annual dividend by the current price of a share.

Column 4: This shows the price-to-earnings ratio (P/E), which is determined by dividing a stock's price by the company's latest 12-month earnings per share. Some people believe a high price-to-earnings figure means that a share is overvalued.

Column 5: This shows volume (VOL), which represents the total number of shares traded (in hundreds).

Column 6: This shows the last trade price for a share at the end (the "close") of the previous trading day.

Column 7: This shows CHG, or change, which is the net change from the last trade price on the previous day and the last price on the preceding day. An up or down arrow may be used to represent whether the change was positive (+) or negative (-).

After you have followed the shares for 10 days, ask yourself: Do these shares seem to be rising or falling? Do they seem like a good investment? What might be affecting the value of these shares? These are the sorts of questions people ask when choosing which shares to invest in.

Other investments

The investments that have been discussed so far are some of the most common, but there are many more ways to invest money.

Some people invest in things that seem more "real" than shares. They might buy a house or a block of flats, in the hope of reselling at a profit in the future. Or they might buy precious metals or even works of art.

There are markets similar to share and bond markets for some other investments. For example, people can invest in a fund that will rise if the price of an agricultural product, such as grains or pigs, rises. They can also invest in a foreign **currency** and hope that its value will rise compared to other currencies.

Propety

Property as a financial investment ranges from buying shopping centres and industrial factories to buying flats or houses. It is also possible to invest in property funds. But the most common property investment occurs when people buy a home for themselves. Some people do not think of a house as an investment. Rather, they think of it as a place to live. But historically, buying a house has been a fairly safe investment. It slowly rises in value over time.

The housing bubble

However, in recent years, people in many countries have invested too much in houses. Interest rates were low in countries such as the United States and United Kingdom in the 2000s, so it became easy to borrow money. Banks began to offer mortgages (loans to buy a home) that did not require a big deposit. Two US government–sponsored agencies made borrowing easier and made more money available for mortgages. They are called Fannie Mae (for the Federal National Mortgage Association) and Freddie Mac (for Federal Home Loan Mortgage Corporation). The extra money and lending made possible by Fannie and Freddie helped lots of low-income families in the United States buy homes, and this bigger demand added to the rise in house prices. These people were often loaned money to buy homes they could not afford.

House prices began to rise more quickly than usual, allowing people to buy a house, then resell it for a large profit. Many people believed that house prices could only go up. Soon millions of people were buying houses as money-making investments.

House prices spiralled higher and higher, until they finally became too expensive for many people to buy. Since housing prices had become so high for no good reason, people called the housing market a "bubble" that would soon "burst". People began falling behind on their mortgage payments. The people who had bought houses in the hopes of reselling them for a profit were unable to find buyers. Many people ended up with mortgages they could not afford, and millions of people lost their homes. (If a person cannot pay back a loan, the lender gains possession of the home.)

Housing investment pluses and minuses

In a normal market, is buying a house a good investment? That depends on the individual. Earlier in life, you may find it better to rent, because young people tend to move more frequently as they change jobs or look for the perfect place to settle down.

Lessons from the housing market

The rise and fall of the housing market in the first decade of this century holds many lessons. The first is that for most people, a house should be thought of as a place to live more so than as an investment. Second, doing what everyone else is doing is often not a good investment strategy. Many people bought homes because they wanted to make money by developing them, or buying and reselling property for a profit. However, at that point there were many buyers in the market, pushing up the price. A better strategy might be to buy something that other people are not buying. In that case, the price may be low and have a better chance of rising over time.

Buying a house also requires paying thousands of pounds as a deposit – money that could perhaps be better invested somewhere else. And unlike other investments, it can be very difficult to sell a home quickly if you need the money.

For people planning to stay in one place for more than five years, a house can be a good investment. While rents increase, a homeowner with a fixed interest mortgage usually has a set payment to make until the mortgage is paid. In some countries, owning a home also offers tax advantages.

Some people buy houses and flats in order to rent them out. If the amount charged for rent is more than the mortgage payment, this can be a good investment. But investors also need to remember that being a landlord can be a lot of work!

Trading currencies

Another form of investment is currency trading. This is done through the worldwide foreign exchange market, which is used by companies and financial institutions to trade currency. Some people will invest in a foreign currency by trading the local currency for foreign currency. If the foreign currency grows in value compared to the local currency, the investor will have made money.

For example, assume you own euros and believe the pound is about to increase in value compared to the euro. You can use your euros to buy pounds at the existing exchange rate. Assume that €1 can be converted into £1. This means that you can convert €100 into £100 (not including the fees for buying and selling currencies). Assume that after using your €100 to buy the £100, the value of pounds does increase relative to euros, with £100 now worth €125. You have made €25 minus your fees from your **speculation**, which is the risk you took with the hope of gain.

But speculation on currency is risky and requires a lot of information and luck. The value of the pound could have fallen relative to the euro, and you would have lost money.

Gold

Gold is a popular investment when people are worried that currency might lose some of its value. Since gold has been traded for thousands of years, people think of it as an investment that holds its value. But like any other, it can be a poor investment if it is too expensive at the time it is bought.

Investors can make money if the currency they have gains in value compared to other currencies.

Speculating in commodities

Investors can also speculate on products called **commodities**—for example, agricultural products, such as wheat and corn, as well as on other things, such as cattle, pigs, metals, oil, coffee, and cocoa. They do this in commodity markets, sometimes referred to as futures markets. A commodity market for a certain type of wheat, for example, estimates the future price for the wheat. If an investor buys a contract to purchase the wheat at that price, and the price ends up being higher, then the investor can sell the contract for a profit. Prices for many of these commodities are greatly affected by weather, as weather affects harvests. World demand also affects the prices of commodities.

One effect of a market like this is that it can increase today's price for a product. For example, by the end of the first decade of this century, many people expected oil prices to keep rising. People traded for the chance to buy oil in the future, when they thought prices would be even higher. This belief actually had the effect of raising the price of oil. Believing that oil would be even more expensive tomorrow, people were willing to pay more for it today.

People can invest in agricultural products like pigs, too.

Diversification and compound interest

Financial markets are the core of a productive economy. They bring together people who are saving with people who can use those savings to invest in the future. As a result, more money is earned and more products are created. The wealth in the economy increases.

Just as financial markets increase the wealth in the economy, they can also increase your wealth if you know how to use them.

Understanding your goals

Saving and investing may reduce the amount of money you have available to spend in the short run, but it can greatly increase the amount you have to spend over your lifetime. How much you should save and how you should invest depends on your particular situation, objectives, and goals. Also, the financial products most appropriate for you depend on your purpose for saving and your tolerance for risk.

For example, money that will be needed for a house deposit in 10 years should be invested differently than money that will be needed for retirement in 50 years. Whatever your situation or objectives, though, you will be more successful in realizing your financial goals if you understand the importance of **diversification** and **compound interest**.

A diversified portfolio

Diversification means reducing risk by holding a number of shares from different corporations (remember umbrella and suncream shares?) or by holding several different financial instruments in your **portfolio**. (Your portfolio is your group of investments.) There is no way to completely eliminate the risk of losing money. But, through diversification, such risks can be lowered.

Company shares

In past years, many employers have encouraged their employees to invest in company shares as a way of showing commitment to the company. However, this can be a very dangerous investment strategy. Investing heavily in any one company is always risky (see page 27). In addition, if the company goes out of business, you may both lose your investment and be out of a job!

Many people try to reduce risk by investing in a mix of shares, bonds, and other financial products. For people seeking to use their money soon, such as those who are close to retirement age, a financial portfolio may include lots of bonds and savings in ISAs, which are less likely to decrease in value. Those who will not use the money for many years are more likely to focus on shares, which are riskier but usually make more money in the long run than other investments.

Diversified investment portfolios range from conservative to aggressive. The most aggressive investor might have all of his or her savings in shares. At the opposite end of the spectrum is the most conservative investor, who might have all of his or her savings in bank deposit and time deposit accounts. Examples of what investment portfolios might contain for those who fall in between are illustrated in the pie charts shown to the right.

These pie charts show what investments might be made by a moderately conservative investor (top), a moderate investor (middle), and a moderately aggressive investor (bottom). Aggressive investors put more money into riskier shares, which are likely to earn more money in the long term. Conservative investors will put more money into safer bets such as saving bonds.

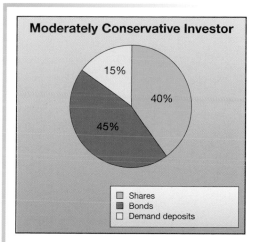

Moderately Conservative Investor

15%
40%
45%

☐ Shares
■ Bonds
☐ Demand deposits

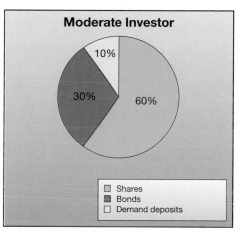

Moderate Investor

10%
30%
60%

☐ Shares
■ Bonds
☐ Demand deposits

Moderately Aggressive Investor

5%
15%
80%

☐ Shares
■ Bonds
☐ Demand deposits

Diversification and individual shares

To reduce risk, an investor may diversify by buying shares in 20 to 30 companies in different industries for which changes in value tend to offset each other.

Think of the example of buying shares of stock in umbrella and suncream companies. Assume that an investment in umbrella shares goes up 40 percent a year when it is raining, and goes down 10 percent a year when the sun is shining. On the other hand, assume that suncream shares goes up 40 percent a year when the sun is shining, and goes down 10 percent a year when it is raining.

Then let's assume that it rains half the year. If you have £100 to invest, you could invest it all in umbrella shares or all in suncream shares, and your expected return would be the same in each case. On average, £100 in umbrella shares would earn £20 for half the year and lose £5 for half the year, for an expected £15, or 15 percent, return. This is the same return you will receive if you invest all of your £100 in suncream shares. But if you invest everything in one industry, your return will tend to be unpredictable, with long periods of losses possible. It could be sunny for quite a long time, and if all your money is invested in umbrella shares, you could lose 10 percent a year. And the same is true if you invest all your money in suncream shares, since it could be rainy for a long time.

Diversifying

Now consider the result of diversifying your investments by putting £50 in umbrella shares and £50 in suncream shares. In this case, you will get the expected return of 15 percent, no matter what the weather is. For example, if it is sunny for the entire year, you earn £20 from the suncream shares and lose £5 from the umbrella shares – for a £15, or 15 percent, return. On the other hand, if it rains for the entire year you earn £20 on your umbrella shares and lose £5 on your suncream shares – for the same £15, or 15 percent, return.

Shares over the long term

While most investors are wise to invest in a variety of financial products, for those people who have a long time to wait for their investment to pay off, shares can be the best investment. Over long periods of time, such as 20 years or more, shares have typically produced better returns than most other investments. Even so, wise investors do careful research before purchasing shares, looking for the best long-term bets. Also, they do not overreact to short-term market fluctuations.

That advice can be hard to swallow during a long downturn. For example, look back at the graph on page 29, showing the rise and fall of the US Dow Jones Industrial Average between 2000 and 2009. Investors who bought shares in 2000 and kept it for 10 years would have found that their shares most likely lost money.

However, looking at share prices over a longer term gives a different picture. Look at this graph, which shows share prices between 1900 and 2009. Over such a long period of time, the ups and downs of the first decade of this century look like a small blip on a steady rise. But sometimes the wait can be too long. Notice that after the stock market crashed beginning in 1929, it took more than 20 years for share prices to recover.

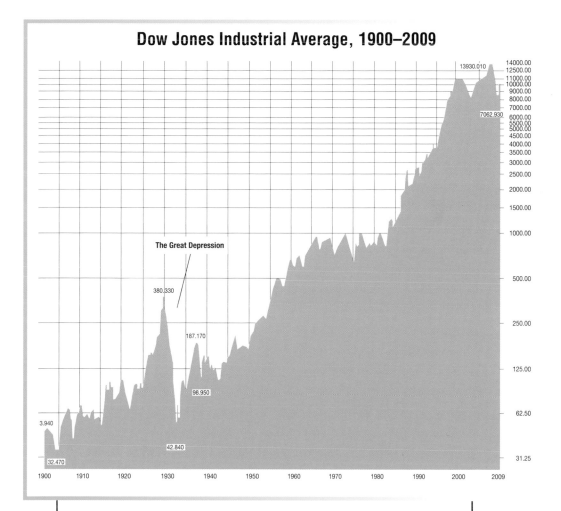

This graph shows the US Dow Jones Industrial Average from 1900 through 2009. Although there have been many dips and falls, the market has always recovered and grown.

Compound interest

Getting the largest return on an investment is clearly important. It may seem as though it takes a stock market wiz to earn a lot of money, but the best strategy is sometimes simply to do nothing. If you invest your money early enough and let it sit and earn interest, your money can grow vastly through the power of compound interest, which is interest received by reinvesting the interest payments you receive.

The secret to benefiting from compound interest is to resist the temptation to spend the returns you earn from your investments. Spending the returns obviously makes sense for an older couple who plan to live off the interest payments of their savings, or off dividends and appreciating investments, during retirement. But when you are young and want your savings and investments to grow, you may want to reinvest the money you make off interest.

Interest on top of interest

By not spending the interest earned on your savings this year, you can add the interest money to your total savings. You will then earn additional interest on this interest the following year. Do the same thing next year and you get interest on your interest on your interest, and so on. At first you will not notice this doing much to increase your wealth. But before long this compounding interest will begin to add up. And the more savings you have, the more interest you are earning to earn interest on, and the faster your savings grow.

Think of it as a small snowball rolling down a snow-covered mountain. Because it starts small, it does not pick up much additional snow (interest) and increases very slowly in size. But as it picks up more snow, it becomes larger and picks up more and more snow, which results in even larger amounts of snow being added to its size. Before long, it is a huge and rapidly growing snowball.

Starting early

It is better to get a late start on a programme of steady saving than never start at all. But because of compound interest, starting early brings great benefits.

Compound interest will not add much to the amount you save right before retirement. But the money you saved years before retirement will have, through compound interest, accumulated and become a truly impressive amount of money by the time you retire. If you start the snowball near the bottom of the mountain, it will still be small when it stops rolling. It is the snowball that started rolling at the top of the mountain that is huge when it gets to the bottom.

Every little bit counts

The power of compound interest can be illustrated with a simple example. Assume a young woman named Katie is considering eliminating the soft drinks, sweets, and crisps she buys every day. Instead, she will invest this money (£5 a day), starting on her 16th birthday.

If Katie decides against having these snacks every day, she will save £1,825 a year. Instead of spending this savings, Katie invests it in a unit trust that provides an annual return of 6 percent a year in real terms – that is, after accounting for **inflation**. (Inflation is how it takes more money over time to buy the same amount of goods and services.) If Katie keeps this up for 10 years, she will have saved £18,250 by her 26th birthday. In addition to this, she will have accumulated £24,055 through compound interest. (We are assuming that she chose to have all of her returns reinvested, to take advantage of compound interest.)

By skipping small purchases such as snacks and investing the money instead, an investor can build up a lot of money over time.

Staying the course

The amount Katie has saved and the amount her savings are worth at each of several points over the rest of her life, beginning with age 26, are shown on this graph. As you can see, at age 26, Katie gains from compound interest has barely achieved lift-off. However, by continuing her saving plan, leaving all her return invested until she turns 36, Katie will have saved £36,508, but will have accumulated a total of £67,134. Continuing until her 46th birthday, Katie will have saved £56,575 and accumulated £144,281. The effect of compound interest has clearly accelerated. And now the benefits really start kicking in.

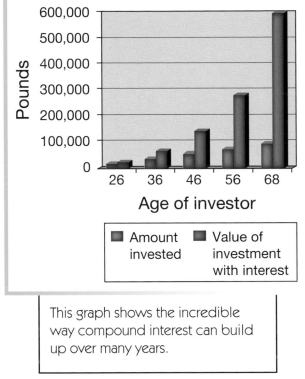

This graph shows the incredible way compound interest can build up over many years.

By the time Katie is 56 she will have accumulated £282,441 from saving contributions of only £73,000. And when she retires at age 68, she will have £599,114 from saving contributions of less than one-sixth that amount, or £94,900. Thus, by choosing not to eat and drink snack foods every day and taking advantage of the power of compound interest, Katie has accumulated about £600,000 in retirement funds!

An expensive delay

The example of Katie can also be used to illustrate the importance of starting a saving programme early. Assume that Katie had bought her daily £5 snacks from ages 16 to 26, only then starting to save instead of snacking. It is good that she started her savings plan, and she will still benefit from the savings. But by postponing her saving programme by 10 years, instead of having £599,114 on her 68th birthday, Katie would have £321,110. Delaying a 52-year saving programme by 10 years reduces Katie's wealth at retirement by £278,004.

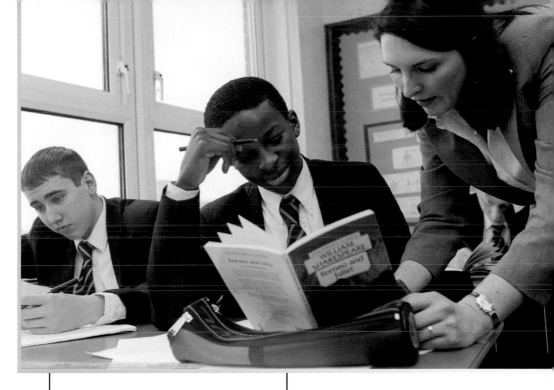

Many teachers rely on pensions as investments for their retirement.

Pensions

Many people do not make their own decisions about how to invest. Instead, their employer offers them a **pension**. This is a fund that a company invests in on behalf of workers. When workers retire, they are entitled to income earned by the fund. Often the income is paid in fixed amounts.

Pensions can be safer than a personal investment plan because they offer a fixed income rather than an income that depends on the market. However, when people managing pension funds make risky investments, they can put the employees that depend on them at risk. Even though some pensions are guaranteed amounts, other companies have reduced pension benefits for their employees when their investments did poorly.

Many companies have found that the money they owe employees is greater than the money that the pension plan is earning as an investment. As a result, some companies have stopped guaranteeing the amount of money an employee will make when he or she retires, instead making it dependent on the value of the fund.

Market volatility and emotions

In the example of Katie's investment programme on pages 41 to 42, it is assumed there will be the same return each year. However, because stock markets are volatile, investing in individual shares will not always give you the same return. The ups and downs – the profits and losses – of the market can result in you having more or less money than Katie had after 52 years of investing. This is true even if you followed the same investment programme she did and the market increased by the same amount.

Stock market trading floors are full of drama and excitement due to the volatility of the prices.

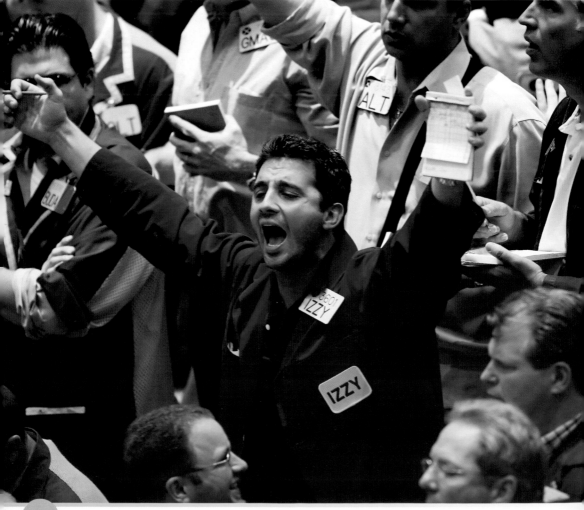

The effect of stock market increases

For example, if the market did not increase at all the first 50 years of your investment programme, but increased so rapidly in the last two years that it caught up with the increase Katie experienced, then all the return would have occurred when you had a lot of money invested. In this case, you would end up with more than Katie.

On the other hand, if the market did all of its increasing over the first two years of your investment programme, and then stayed the same for the next 50 years, all the return would have come when you had very little invested. In this case, you would end up with less than Katie. These are extreme examples, but they illustrate that the timing of stock market increases can affect the return you receive.

Emotional ups and downs

The biggest problem with the ups and downs of the stock market is that it can cause investors to experience emotional ups and downs. These emotional swings often affect a person's investment decisions in a harmful way. Instead of staying with a steady investment programme like Katie did, there is a strong tendency for people to buy and sell shares in response to emotions - and this usually results in them getting a much smaller return than Katie received.

Timing the market

Because no one can know what the stock market will do in the short run, the best strategy for most people when investing in shares is to stay with a steady programme of buying, like Katie. It is not wise to try to "time the market" by moving in and out. As we have seen, the stock market generally gives investors a higher return than other investments over the long term. Also, when you keep investing during stock market declines, you are benefiting from the opportunity to buy shares even more cheaply than if the stock market were not falling.

Fear of a downturn

When the stock market is dropping and people see the value of their investments getting smaller and smaller, it is natural for them to get worried. Markets can continue on a downward trend for a few years before starting to recover, with a full recovery sometimes taking even more years.

As the markets decline over time, worry can turn into panic, at which time a lot of people sell their shares and put their money in safer (more predictable) financial products, like savings bonds or savings accounts. But this is often about the time the stock market starts its recovery and starts paying higher returns than the safer investments.

Fear of missing an upturn

Emotions can also motivate unfortunate investment decisions when the stock market is increasing. People who have sold their shares at a large loss are understandably reluctant to repeat the experience, and so they tend to stay out of the market – and in their safe investments – as the stock market begins to head back up.

But if the stock market continues to rise, there will be news reports about all the money being made in shares. These news reports will be supported (and often exaggerated) by comments from friends and associates about how well they are doing in the stock market. Before long, these reports can cause the fear of losing money in shares to be gradually replaced by the fear of being left behind. The result is often that the people who sold shares when share prices were at or near their lowest point jump back into the stock market when prices are at or near a peak.

US Federal Reserve Chairman Alan Greenspan worried that US investors were suffering from "irrational exuberance". He felt that people were buying dot-com shares based on emotion rather than common sense.

"Irrational exuberance"

In the late 1990s, the rise of Internet-related shares led to what many people later saw as emotional investments. The promise of the Internet led many people to believe that new Internet companies (also known as "dot-coms", after their web addresses) would be very profitable. Investors seemed to be offering money to anyone who had an idea for a new online business, and soon those businesses began offering shares. People raced to be the first ones to snatch up the shares, sending share prices higher. However, many of these companies had little money or experience, and no real plan for making a profit.

As share prices rose higher and higher, Alan Greenspan, chairman of the US central bank, the Federal Reserve, commented that many investors were too optimistic and may be suffering from "irrational exuberance", meaning they were overly excited without really looking closely at the facts. He was proven right when shares crashed in what was known as the bursting of the "dot-com bubble". Some companies saw their share prices tumble, while other companies disappeared entirely. US companies such as Pets.com spent millions on advertising, only to run out of money soon after. Lastminute.com in the United Kingdom saw its share price go from around £5 per share to 18p per share. It was soon clear that the mania over dot-com stocks was truly irrational.

Investing during downturns

In 1929 John Raskob, an executive with the US car company General Motors, was interviewed for the magazine *Ladies' Home Journal.* In the interview, Raskob recommended a steady programme of investing in shares, predicting that this would return 24 percent a year over the next 20 years. The article containing Raskob's recommendation was published a few weeks before the start of the worst stock market decline in US history, known as the Great Depression.

Over the next three years, the shares on the New York Stock Exchange declined by 89 percent, as measured by the Dow Jones Industrial Average (see the graph on page 39). But despite the ridicule Raskob received for his comments in the article, his advice was actually good – even if his prediction was overly optimistic.

An investor who began investing just US$15 each month (the amount Raskob suggested) in the stock market, beginning when Raskob's advice was published, would have done better after four years than the person who had invested the same amount in US Treasury bills (the safest US government bonds). In 20 years, the investor would have had US$9,000 in wealth (far more than the Treasury bill investor), and in 30 years he or she would have had over US$60,000 (having saved only US$5,400 to buy shares).

This represents an annual return of 13 percent for 30 years. This is less than the 24 percent Raskob predicted, but still a return far greater than what would have been received by those who avoided the stock market crash by investing in low-risk government bonds instead of shares.

During the Great Depression, millions of people found themselves out of work and sometimes living on the streets.

Young investors

When you are young, it is a good idea to start with an investment portfolio with many different kinds of shares. This allows you to take advantage of the higher long-run returns from shares.

Young people can even do well during bad periods for investors. For example, from 1929 until the early 1930s there was a sharp drop, or crash, in the stock market known as the Great Depression (see box on page 48). Whereas the crash was a disaster for investors who were nearing retirement age, young people could have seen this as a tremendous opportunity rather than a loss. They would have had very little invested in the stock market, or anywhere else, when they were just starting their investment programme. They could have bought shares at very cheap prices and been able to hold onto the shares for the long term, into their retirement.

Taking advantage of financial markets

The old saying is true—money does make the world go around. Financial markets are critical to the functioning of the global economy. They keep the wheels of business turning. And if you invest wisely, they can improve your life by earning you money for the future.

Financial markets benefit you every day. They make it easier for suppliers to produce the goods consumers like you want now, to anticipate what you will want in the future, and to make the goods available at reasonable prices. These markets also provide you with opportunities to contribute to this productive process, by channelling your savings into their most valuable uses.

Saving, not spending

The best advice to earn money is both the simplest and the most difficult. It all comes down to saving rather than spending. The money you save and invest today is likely to grow greatly over time. By carefully saving and investing your money, you can take full advantage of the opportunities offered by the many forms of investment offered in the world today.

Fact file

The following chart summarizes some of the main forms of investments covered in this book. Look back on the pages shown to review each type of investment.

DIFFERENT KINDS OF INVESTMENTS	
Form of investment	**What it does**
Current account (page 14)	Keeps money conveniently available, but it may not earn any money
Instant access savings account (page 15)	Money can be withdrawn when you need it, but it earns money slowly
Notice savings account (page 16)	Makes more than a savings account, but money is less available for use
ISA (page 16)	Can save taxes on savings, but has an upper limit
Savings bond (page 22)	Earns a moderate amount of money, with a small risk of losing money
Shares (page 24)	Can earn or lose a lot of money
Property (houses and flats) (page 32)	Usually rises in value (worth) over time, but is expensive and takes time to resell
Commodities such as gold, oil, or wheat (page 35)	Value can rise or fall due to weather and world events that affect supply and demand

Risk-return pyramid

This pyramid shows the risks and rewards of various investments. Investments at the bottom have lower risk, but they also tend to offer lower rewards over the long term. Investments at the top have higher risk, but they also potentially offer greater rewards over the long term.

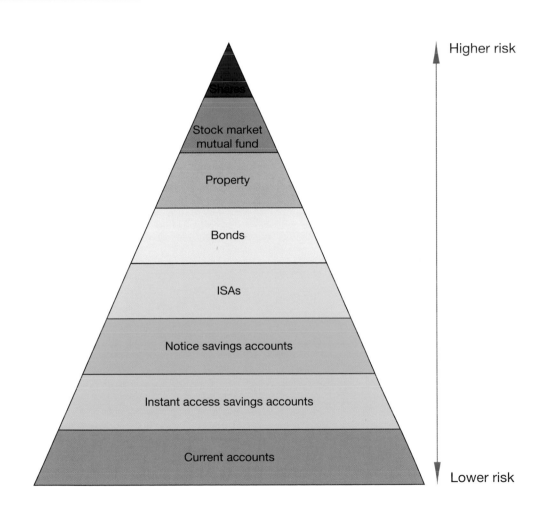

Higher risk

Shares

Stock market mutual fund

Property

Bonds

ISAs

Notice savings accounts

Instant access savings accounts

Current accounts

Lower risk

Stock market returns

The graph below shows the rise in the stock market over more than 100 years, as measured by the US Dow Jones Industrial Average. Although there were long periods of decline, such as from 1929 to 1931, overall the market has risen over time.

Although the stock market can rise over the very long term, it can also go through periods of extreme volatility, a fact reflected in the far-right section of this graph. As this shows, the stock market had moments of dipping dramatically throughout the first decade of the century.

Dow Jones Industrial Average, 1900–2009

Glossary

appreciate when the value or price of something, such as shares, bonds, property, art, or diamonds, increases

asset item of value

bond investment that is a loan to the organization that sold it to you – usually a company or a national government – that pays a specified interest rate until a stated date

central bank country's main bank, which has the power to regulate financial matters

commodity product, such as oil, gold, or wheat, that can be traded

compound interest interest earned by reinvesting the interest payments received

consumer anyone who uses (consumes) a resource, good, or service

credit paying for an expense with borrowed money

credit rating agency company that rates investments on their level of risk

currency money

debt money owed

default failure to repay

demand quantity of a good that consumers are willing and able to buy

deposititor person who pays money into an account

depreciate when the value or price of something, such as shares, bonds, property, art, or diamonds, decreases

direct debit ability of a third party to deduct money on a regular basis from someone else's account, with that person's permission. The amount may vary from month to month, for example, in payment for a mobile phone bill.

diversification reducing risk by holding a number of shares from different companies

dividend part of a profit that companies pay directly to shareholders (people who own shares in the company)

economy structures that shape the financial life of a country

good tangible item that provides value, such as a car

income earnings

inflation rise in the general price of goods and services

interest payment received in exchange for loaning money to someone; also, a payment owed in exchange for borrowing money from someone

interest rate amount of interest paid or received over the course of a year, as a percentage of the amount borrowed or loaned. For example, if you borrow £100 and pay £10 in interest at the end of the year, the interest rate is 10 percent.

invest lending money with the expectation of receiving benefits or rewards in the future

investment money given with the expectation of receiving benefits or reward in the future

investor anyone who lends money with the expectation of receiving benefits or rewards in the future

loan money borrowed with repayment conditions

loss used to describe when a person loses money on an investment

market place where people buy and sell goods and services. It can be a specific location, like your corner shop, or it can be as extensive as the global market for oil.

maturity date at which an investment is ready to be paid

mortgage loan to buy a home

pension fund that a company invests in on behalf of workers, to be paid when the workers retire

portfolio individual's investments, including such things as savings accounts, shares, and bonds he or she owns

price amount charged for a good or service

producer person involved in creating goods and services

profit money made minus the cost of expenses

recession when an economy's growth slows down

return earnings received from an investment

risk chance that something will turn out differently than expected

savings amount of money a person receives and puts away, rather than spending

service performed action that has value, such as a haircut or having a car repaired

share unit of ownership in a public company; also called a stock

speculation financial risk taken with the hope of gain

standing order request made by you to a bank or building society to pay a specific amount on a specific date into someone else's account, for example, as a monthly rent payment

supply quantity of a good or service that a business produces

time deposit investment that earns a fixed interest rate over a specified time period

unit trust group of investments made by a financial services company on behalf of many investors

value benefit received from a good or service. Money is a common measure of value.

volatility changeability; changing a lot

Find out more

Books to read

Ankrum, Sharon. *History in Literature: The Story Behind John Steinbeck's Of Mice and Men (Great Depression)*. Oxford: Heinemann Library, 2006

Downing, David. *Political and Economic Systems: Capitalism*. Oxford: Heinemann Library, 2008

Hall, Alvin. *Show Me the Money*. London: Dorling Kindersley, 2008

Hollander, Barbara. *Life Skills: Managing Money*. Oxford: Heinemann Library, 2009

Hollander, Barbara. *Life Skills: Raising Money*. Oxford: Heinemann Library, 2009

Websites

This is the website of the Economics, Business, and Enterprise Association. It is a professional association for anyone interested in teaching and studying economics.
www.ebea.org.uk

This website provides personal finance information for young adults ages 14 through 24 who live in the United Kingdom.
www.doughuk.com

This is the official site of the London Stock Exchange.
www.londonstockexchange.com

This is the official site of the UK National Savings and Investments.
www.nsandi.com

Index